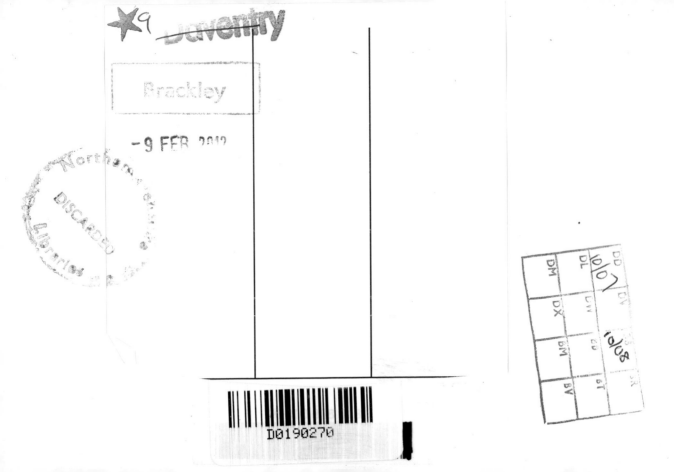

The Lifeboats
Story

Coxswain Robert Harland of Whitby in 1934 with a young admirer. (Photo Press)

Southwold Lifeboat crew put their Atlantic 75 through its paces. (Nicholas Leach)

The Lifeboats Story

Edward Wake-Walker

Sutton Publishing

First published in the United Kingdom in 2007 by
Sutton Publishing, an imprint of NPI Media Group Limited
Cirencester Road · Chalford · Stroud · Gloucestershire · GL6 8PE

in association with the Royal National Lifeboat Institution

British Library Cataloguing in Publication Data
A catalogue record for this book is available from the British
Library.

Hardback ISBN 978-0-7509-4858-6

➤

*Penlee's Severn class
lifeboat (Ivan Ellen) on
exercise near St Michael's
Mount, Cornwall.
(Nicholas Leach)*

CONTENTS

ACKNOWLEDGEMENTS

My grateful thanks go to those at the RNLI who helped me to gather material for this book, especially James Vaughan, Carol Waterkeyn, Eleanor Driscoll, Derek King and Nathan Williams.

I am also indebted to all those photographers who have allowed their work to be used to help tell the story.

The biggest thank-you goes, though, to all the RNLI who are working hard to ensure that there will be many more chapters to add to the remarkable story of the lifeboats far into the future.

To find out how you can become involved, visit www.rnli.org.uk

Credit has been given where it is known but the RNLI would be grateful for any information where errors or gaps remain.

St David's all-weather Tyne class, Garside, at full speed off the Pembrokeshire coast. (Nigel Millard)

There are still plenty of seaside holiday-makers and even some boat owners who are only dimly aware of the 180-year-old voluntary rescue service, primed to race to their assistance should the need arise. More than 230 lifeboat stations line the coast of the United Kingdom and Ireland operating high-powered craft from a 5m inflatable to a 17m all-weather boat. Their crews answer more than 8,000 calls each year and rescue, on average, twenty-one individuals every day. Search-and-rescue cover is guaranteed in all conditions up to 100 miles off shore, whether it is for a lone yachtsman or a 40,000-ton freighter wallowing in 30ft waves. Even the beach-goer nowadays is served by the Royal National Lifeboat Institution which has set up its own system of lifeguard patrols on some of the more dangerous beaches in the UK.

Not many people ventured close to the rugged shores of Britain 300 years ago. Few could swim and the ocean was widely feared for its ability to swallow up those who failed to heed its mysterious power. Even the most hardened seafarers made their final approaches to a British or Irish

Bamburgh Castle, Northumberland, where the first unsinkable boat, specially adapted for lifesaving, was stationed in 1786.

port with trepidation. Too many of their fellows had been frozen to death on an off-lying sandbank, bludgeoned to oblivion on a rocky reef or drowned under a towering cliff.

For those small, defiant communities that looked to the sea for a livelihood of sorts, the winter storms, which threatened their fishermen and brought them hunger and misery, could also occasionally offer up a grim harvest. When the morning light revealed the silhouette of a splintered mast and a mangled hull hard against the nearby headland, many would hope that any life on board had already been extinguished. Here was a chance to deny the sea a prized cargo and to put bread in the children's mouths. Compassion for the crew who might still be clinging to the rigging was an almost unaffordable luxury, although to reach them and to have them away from the scene could often make the business of salvage less complicated.

Motives for rescue, even in those hard times, were not always mercenary; when thirteen warships off the coast of Kent succumbed to the Great Storm of 1703, one Deal lugger put out and brought 63 survivors ashore while other local boats saved a further 200. Even then, though, the story goes that it was the town's tradesmen,

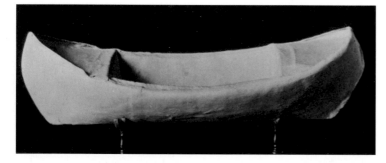

The tin model of a lifeboat that won William Wouldhave half the prize money in the 1789 competition to design a lifeboat.

not its boatmen, who reached the survivors stranded on the Goodwin Sands, the latter being too busy with a salvaging bonanza.

By the end of the eighteenth century, with Britain the undisputed hub of the commercial world, the approaches to London, Liverpool, Glasgow, Newcastle, Cardiff, Dublin and many other ports were thick with masts and sails, each vessel a potential victim of the winds and tides on which they depended for their trade. Now, though, when a ship hit the rocks – and it happened more than 1,000 times a year – there were often people with rounder stomachs who witnessed the disaster. These were citizens of coastal towns and cities who had grown rich on the proceeds of maritime trade, some who might even have held a stake in her misfortune, and they viewed the wreck with a very different mixture of emotions from the impoverished fisher folk.

The prudent ones could well have felt relief that they had shared their risk of loss at Lloyd's, the London underwriters. Several, though, began to agonise over the plight of the crewmen, often plainly visible

'It was now about 9 o'clock, and several boats were heard at a short distance from the ship; but they rendered no assistance to the distressed on board. Whether this was owing to their being employed in the humane purpose of saving those who had clung to pieces of wreck (upon which many had ventured from the vessel), or because they were engaged in plunder, is a matter which has not been ascertained.'

Thomas Gilpin, fourth mate and survivor of the wreck of the *Earl of Abergavenny*, off the Dorset coast, February 1805

Did you know?
A wooden dipper used by a woman drawing water from a well which always came back upright gave William Wouldhave the idea for his self-righting lifeboat model.

A memorial at South Shields to William Wouldhave, whose model inspired the self-righting lifeboat. (Robin Sharpe)

from the shore, dropping to their deaths from the rigging. What could be done, they started to ask one another, to prevent so many shipwrecks and to offer some chance of rescue to their victims?

Of course, there were occasions when small local boats could be used to ferry survivors ashore when the conditions allowed. The earliest mention of a vessel set aside specifically for saving human life appears in the Liverpool municipal records in March 1777 giving instructions for repairs to be carried out to 'the boat, which was formerly ordered to be built and kept at Formby in readiness to fetch any shipwrecked persons from the banks'. Unfortunately little more is known about this boat or its usefulness other than it was 'stationed on the strand about a mile below Formby lower landmark' and that it was in the charge of a Richard Scarisbrick. Could he hold a claim to being the world's first lifeboat coxswain?

A few years earlier, in 1772, the Bishop of Durham, Nathaniel Crewe, died and a trust was established in his name to address the growing problem of shipwrecks and their tragic consequences on the Northumberland coast. One of its administrators, Dr John Sharp, Archdeacon of Northumberland, set up a lookout system at Bamburgh Castle with its view over the dreaded Farne Islands, whereby horsemen were sent out on patrol when the wind got up to look for ships in trouble. In 1786 the trust asked a London inventor and coachbuilder, Lionel Lukin, to apply a method he had developed of making a vessel unsinkable by the use of cork and watertight buoyancy chambers, to one of their local cobles. It was put to good use as a rescue boat for several years at Bamburgh.

The claim inscribed on Lukin's grave in St Leonard's churchyard in Hythe, Kent, to be 'the first to build a Lifeboat' has always had to contend with two other carved memorials, both hundreds of miles

Did you know?
Sir William Hillary, founder of the RNLI, won three Gold Medals for bravery aboard the lifeboat at Douglas, Isle of Man.

further north. One, in the grounds of St Hilda's Church, South Shields, proclaims that William Wouldhave, buried there,

Did you know?
The RNLI, founded
in 1824, is the oldest
lifeboat service in
the world.

was 'Inventor of the Invaluable Blessing to Mankind, The Lifeboat'. Wouldhave's involvement came about after a tragedy in the mouth of the Tyne in 1789. A group of South Shields businessmen had been among the crowds who witnessed the drowning of all aboard the wrecked *Adventure* in a storm. Shocked by their powerlessness to assist, they arranged a competition to find the best plan of a rescue boat that could be used the next time such a disaster struck.

Some rancour followed the result of the competition when the winner, William Wouldhave, was only offered half the two-guinea prize money (which contemptuously he refused). His tin model, which suggested a design that would neither sink, go to pieces, nor lie bottom-up, was given to Henry Greathead, an unsuccessful entrant and local boat-builder, to produce in full-scale reality, incorporating the best features of Wouldhave's and other designs submitted to the competition.

The resulting lifeboat, not self-righting but still unsinkable, came to be known as the 'Original'. She rapidly proved herself and, along with improved successors, acted as a catalyst in the formation of a national lifeboat service. (Greathead's was the third headstone to claim the invention as his.) Now that a boat existed which gave sufficient confidence to rescuers to take on heavy surf and high winds, local societies were being formed to operate one themselves.

Lloyd's of London, showing an appropriate concern for the welfare of seafarers, encouraged the setting up of stations and funded fourteen Greathead boats. Douglas on the Isle of Man acquired its own lifeboat in 1802 and here an eccentric baronet who loved adventure became a member of the crew. In Sir William Hillary there was at last someone who had direct experience of the horrors of shipwreck and who also carried

A model of the 'Original'.

An early line-throwing mortar, often the only means of reaching a wreck from the shore before lifeboats became commonplace. (Associated Press Ltd)

A contemporary etching of Henry Greathead's 'Original', which gave forty years' service at the mouth of the Tyne. She was finally wrecked in 1830 with the loss of two of her crew.

The Gold Medal of the RNLI, showing the head of Sir William Hillary. The medal has been awarded 119 times for gallantry since 1824 and only 8 times in the past 50 years.

influence in royal and establishment circles. His vision was to establish a nationwide organisation which not only provided coastal communities with rescue boats and rocket lines, but one that would also reward volunteer lifesavers with money and medals and recompense their widows should they come to grief. He realised that until salvage ceased to be the only financial incentive for putting out to a wreck, people would continue to die unnecessarily.

In 1823 he published a pamphlet which proposed a 'National Institution for the Preservation of Life from Shipwreck'. The following year, with the support of MPs, the Archbishop of Canterbury, the Lord Mayor of London and others, a lifeboat service came into being relying, as it does to this day, wholly on voluntary contributions.

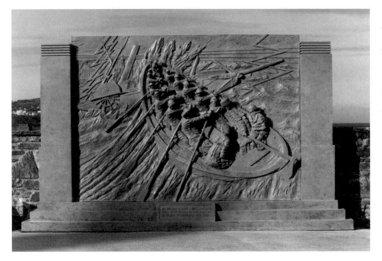

It is still possible to see a Greathead-designed lifeboat. She is the *Zetland*, the oldest lifeboat still in existence, on display on the seafront of Redcar in Cleveland. She served the town from 1802 to 1864, saving more than 500 lives, and is very similar to The Original, 30ft in length and with six pairs of oars. Her bow and stern rise sharply like the segment of a melon and are both pointed so that her crew can row her in either direction without needing to turn the boat in heavy seas. She has no rudder and is steered, instead, with an oar. Cork along the gunwale, cork lining and cork-filled cases make her the most buoyant vessel of her age.

The design of this boat was, however, too original for some of the boatmen of the British Isles. At a number of places Greathead boats had been enthusiastically purchased and almost instantly neglected. Even if locals were now being encouraged to put out to the rescue, they preferred to place their trust in their own boats rather than use this alien and unwieldy-looking craft.

In 1804 at Bawdsey in Suffolk, where, three years earlier, no less a figure than Lord Nelson had contributed five guineas

The Zetland, built in 1802 to Greathead's design, served Redcar for sixty-two years and saved more than 500 lives.

The brigatine *Jeune Hortense stranded in Mounts Bay in May 1888. The Penzance lifeboat* Dora *rescued her four-man crew. (James Gibson)*

Did you know?

The port of Fremantle in Western Australia is named after Admiral Sir Charles Fremantle who, earlier in his life, became the first person to win an RNLI Gold Medal, plunging into surf at Christchurch, Hampshire, to help a shipwrecked crew in March 1824.

another Greathead boat stood idle, felt the design unsuitable for their conditions. Apart from wanting something with a flatter bottom and weightier build to cope with the sudden heavy seas whipped up by gales in their comparatively shallow waters, they wanted to be able to sail their lifeboat as well as row her.

A firm believer in listening to the locals, Lionel Lukin, recruited by the newly-formed Suffolk Humane Society, worked with a Lowestoft boat-builder to make an unsinkable version of the local pilot and salvage boats for the town. The result, in 1807, was the 40ft *Frances Ann* which gave distinguished service for more than forty years, saving 300 lives and inspiring the Norfolk and Suffolk type of lifeboat, widely used on the East Anglian coast throughout the nineteenth century.

towards the cost of a Greathead boat, a naval lieutenant and a crew of coastguardsmen launched the lifeboat and saved seven crewmen and a woman from the brig *Pallas*, wrecked on passage between the Tyne and the Thames. But this still did not impress the local beach men who, along with the boatmen of Lowestoft where

Henry Richardson, one of the contenders in the Duke of Northumberland's 1851 competition, produced a design comprising two iron tubes meeting fore and aft with a raft structure on top. Although the tubular lifeboat was not widely favoured, the design was used successfully for more than thirty-five years by the crews at Rhyl, North Wales, and here at New Brighton, Merseyside.

Another man who realised the advantage of a lifeboat with both oars and sails was George Palmer, MP, one of the early members of the Committee of Management of the 'Shipwreck Institution', as the RNLI was colloquially known in those days. He used the experience of his younger days at sea to design a 28ft 8in pulling and sailing boat using air-cases for additional buoyancy and costing only £60 to build. With a shortage of funds becoming a crucial issue for the Shipwreck Institution all too soon after its eager inauguration, Palmer's lifeboat was a less expensive alternative and some forty-five were ordered by the Institution between 1825 and 1850 and sent as far afield as Arklow in Ireland, Stromness in the Orkneys and the Isles of Scilly. A batch was even ordered by the French Minister of Marine for use across the Channel.

With the decline in the Institution's fortunes in the second quarter of the nineteenth century came a period when there was little centralised leadership in the business of ensuring lifeboats were ready for action around the coast. The Committee of Management continued to make awards and confer bravery medals when accounts of rescues reached them, but they were seldom carried out in the Institution's boats and by 1838 only 123

Did you know?
During one of the worst storms on record in October 1859, 248 ships were wrecked on the British and Irish coasts and 686 lives lost.

services were recognised, a quarter of the number processed in the early heyday. Annual income had also dwindled from £10,000 in 1825 to a few hundred pounds. The most effective lifeboats were being run by local societies such as at the mouth of the Tyne. In 1839, when the Shipwrecked Fishermen and Mariners Royal Benevolent Society was set up, primarily to care for shipwreck survivors and their families, and also to provide a certain number of lifeboats, a total eclipse of Sir William Hillary's noble creation was threatened.

Then, on 4 December 1849 another disaster at the mouth of the Tyne changed the course of events. *Provident*, one of the two lifeboats kept at South Shields by the Tyne Lifeboat Society, was capsized soon after reaching the wrecked brig, *Betsy*. She had a double crew of twenty-four men, mostly pilots, and all but four of them were drowned. When would-be rescuers lose their lives, the tragedy is felt across the country, especially among seafarers. One man, in particular, was greatly affected by this loss: he was the Fourth Duke of Northumberland.

A seafaring man who had served with distinction as a junior officer under Admiral Collingwood, the Duke was determined to improve the lot, not just of his local lifeboat crews, but of all rescuers. He had just agreed, in 1851, to take up the presidency of the ailing Shipwreck Institution and, as an immediate gesture of his commitment, put up a 100-guinea prize for the best new model of a lifeboat, echoing the exercise of sixty years earlier.

The distinguished panel of naval officers and shipwrights, who considered the 280 entries, paid particular attention to a design's qualities as a rowing and sailing boat in all weathers; its stability, safety and buoyancy at the bow for launching through surf; its means of freeing itself of water; its overall buoyancy; its self-righting ability and its capacity for survivors. Their decision (endorsed at the highest level by the Surveyor of the Navy, Sir Baldwin Wake-Walker) was to award the prize to James Beeching, whose 36ft, twelve-oared, self-righting model came closest to their ideal.

Although a few lifeboats were built to Beeching's plans, the committee asked one of its members, James Peake, to design and build a boat which incorporated the best

Early publicity for the RNLI in the form of a lantern slide using unashamedly emotive imagery.

17

features from all the models submitted. The result was a 30ft self-righter which formed the basis of the fleet for the next fifty years.

The new Beeching and Peake designs were put on show at the Great Exhibition in Hyde Park in the summer of 1851 and attracted much public interest. Now the world could see what the Shipwreck Institution was all about: lifeboats. One of the first of many important reforms brought about by Richard Lewis, the energetic new secretary, was to demonstrate this primary role in a new title, the Royal National Lifeboat Institution.

Under Lewis the RNLI's fortunes were turned round and new boats and equipment began to appear on the coast. While voluntary donations started to grow again, there was a need in 1854 to accept an annual grant from the government to maintain momentum. As the financial situation improved, the grant became more of an impediment than an advantage with its attendant government conditions. An unaided organisation also seemed more attractive to voluntary supporters and it was therefore with considerable satisfaction that the Institution regained its independence from state support in 1869. To this day that status has remained the same.

Although the effect on the RNLI was not immediate, the day in September 1838 when the Longstone lighthouse keeper and his 22-year-old daughter put out in a small coble to reach the survivors of the paddle steamer *Forfarshire* marked a new era of widespread public appreciation of the bravery of rescuers at sea. The event was a terrible tragedy in many ways; most of the passengers and crew were lost soon after the ship hit the rocks of the Farne Islands, Northumberland, and broke in half. While a few crewmen got away in a boat, only thirteen other people, including a woman and her two small children, were left alive on the wreck.

By daylight the next morning, when William Darling and his daughter Grace had spotted the wreck and rowed a mile through rock-strewn waters to save whom they could, the two children had died of exposure, leaving their mother and ten men still alive.

That this forlorn group of survivors owed their lives, in part, at least, to a petite but plucky Northumberland lass was an

Grace Darling and her father William battle to reach the survivors of the Forfarshire *in September 1838.*

20

irresistible story for the early Victorian press and public. An island nation loves to recognise those who pit themselves against its old enemy, the sea, and as the number of shipwreck victims grew, so did the hero-worship of the likes of Grace Darling.

Charles Dickens caught the mood in 1849 with the publication of *David Copperfield* and the tragic death of the character Ham Peggotty in his attempt to rescue the villain Steerforth from a shipwreck. Local and national newspapers began to be filled with stories of wreck-and-rescue and their readers knew that with every storm new accounts of tragic deaths and heroic feats would be served up to them. And in the new post-1850s age of the RNLI the stories increasingly involved their own lifeboats. At last the Silver and Gold Medals of the Institution were being awarded to

Survivors of the Forfarshire are comforted in the safety of Longstone lighthouse.

Coxswain Charles Fish of Ramsgate, hero of the Indian Chief rescue of 1881.

21

Did you know?

Grace Darling died of consumption, aged 29, only six years after her daring rescue mission.

their own retained coxswains and volunteer crews.

When, for instance, the Austrian barque *Pace* was driven ashore on the north Devon coast on 28 December 1868, it was the RNLI's 34ft self-righter *Hope*, based at Appledore, which launched with the aid of horses into the raging surf. On the first attempt, nine people were brought ashore from the wreck at the expense of the lifeboat's rudder which was torn off as the two vessels were thrown together. Joseph Cox, the Appledore coxswain, in spite of an injury received in the same collision, put out to sea again to try to reach the rest of the ship's crew. This time the lifeboat capsized just short of the wreck but all of her crew managed to get back on board and return to shore. Joseph Cox was awarded the Silver Medal for bravery after this rescue.

Thirteen years on, in January 1881, when the *Daily Telegraph* published a graphic account of the epic Gold Medal-winning mission by Coxswain Charles Fish of Ramsgate and his crew to another barque, the *Indian Chief*, disintegrating on the Long Sands off the north Kent coast, readers would no longer need reminding that here

was another extraordinary accomplishment of the RNLI. When wrecks occurred several miles out to sea, it was the practice for Ramsgate's pulling and sailing lifeboat to be towed to the scene by a steam-tug. On this occasion, when the lifeboat arrived it was

The hulk of the Mexico stranded at low tide in the Ribble estuary. Twenty-seven lifeboatmen lost their lives attempting to rescue her crew.

'Oh, sir, she was a noble boat! We could see her crew – twelve of them – sitting on the thwarts, all looking our way, motionless as carved figures, and there was not a stir among them as, in an instant, the boat leapt from the crest of a towering sea, right into the monstrous broken tumble.'

Mate of the *Indian Chief*, wrecked off Ramsgate in January 1881, arrive after a night in the rigging and on seeing the lifeboat

too dark to see the wreck and the only choice for her crew was to ride out the storm at the end of the towline for the night, exposed to the icy gale and gigantic waves. They survived the night and still had the strength to negotiate the treacherous shallows over the sands next morning to rescue the handful of men who had not succumbed to exposure in the tangled rigging.

Then, five years later, in 1886, what began as another triumphant rescue by the Lytham lifeboat in the Ribble Estuary turned into the worst disaster ever experienced by the RNLI, causing the organisation to look carefully at its responsibilities and awakening a new way of raising funds.

Just after 3 o'clock on the morning of Friday 10 December 1886, and to the cheers of a sizeable crowd which had been waiting through the night in the wind and rain, Coxswain Thomas Clarkson had just put ashore the entire twelve-man crew of a German barque *Mexico*, which had run aground on a sandbank. In very heavy breaking seas, caused by a gale from the north-west meeting a powerful ebb tide head on, he and his crew had successfully negotiated the lethal shoals of the estuary and, in spite of a near-capsize, when four oars were broken, had located the wreck in total darkness, got alongside and rescued the crew. He would later be awarded the RNLI Silver Medal for his gallant services that night.

What no one stepping ashore from that lifeboat knew was that two other lifeboats – one from neighbouring St Anne's and another from Southport across the estuary – had also answered the *Mexico's* distress signals and, even before the Lytham boat was back ashore, both had capsized with the loss of twenty-seven men and only two survivors. The disaster provoked a national wave of sympathy for the families of the drowned lifeboatmen and many questions were asked of the RNLI about the safety and operation of their lifeboats, neither of which righted themselves as they should have done.

The Institution looked hard at the procedures for coordinating lifeboat launches and accelerated the building of lifeboats with better stability using water ballast. It also focused minds on alternative means of powering a lifeboat other than by sail and oar. Steam had been in use in vessels for a century – could not lifeboats benefit from such technology?

Ramsgate lifeboat is towed by steam tug close to the wreck of the Indian Chief *before the crew make their final approach under sail across the 'monstrous broken tumble'.*

A lifeboat far from the sea in Salisbury's Castle Street in July 1907 for the Lifeboat Saturday parade. (Peter Daniels)

Did you know?

A pulling lifeboat cost £250 to build in 1852, maybe about £25,000 at today's prices. The modern Tamar class lifeboats cost £2.5 million each to build.

Sir Charles Macara, a wealthy businessman and member of the St Anne's lifeboat committee, who became pivotal during the aftermath of the disaster as anxious relatives waited for news outside his house – the only one in the town fitted with a telephone – harnessed public goodwill by establishing a widows' fund.

After the disaster he wanted to do more for the RNLI and decided that the

Padstow's lifeboat, Arab, built in 1882, rounding Stepper Point in a gale.

London Lifeboat Day, Trafalgar Square, 1932. By the 1930s collectors were almost as familiar a sight as the London bobby. (Keystone View Co)

The Lizard lifeboat Admiral Sir George Back *takes the last men off the barque,* Hansy, *wrecked on her voyage from Sweden to Sydney in 1911 with a cargo of timber.*

A pulling and sailing Watson class lifeboat stationed at Penzance in 1899.

Institution's income was dangerously dependent upon a wealthy but narrow group of subscribers. His idea was to bring the appeal of the lifeboat service to the man in the street – quite literally – by parading an RNLI lifeboat through the streets of Manchester and asking shoppers and onlookers to place their silver and copper donations in purses attached to long poles. The first of these 'Lifeboat Saturdays' took place in 1891 and the idea soon caught on in other large cities throughout Britain. This method of collecting soon evolved into the Lifeboat Flag Day that we know today and is believed by many to have been the original inspiration for all charity street fundraising.

One shocking revelation following the *Mexico* disaster in 1886 was the poor state of health of some of those who put out to the rescue aboard the St Anne's lifeboat. The coxswain of the lifeboat, William Johnson, a 35-year-old fisherman, was very sick with consumption and had not been expected to live longer than a few months. Two or three of the other crew members were also not strong men, one of them having had only 'a basin of gruel all day', apparently stinting himself on behalf of his wife and children.

Poverty was still rife on many parts of the coast at the turn of the nineteenth century and the stampede of local men for the lifeboat at the sound of a distress rocket was often as much about the few shillings they would receive if chosen to man an oar as it was about concern for fellow

A portrait of Coxswain Henry Blogg by Thomas Dugdale.

Henry Blogg won the Silver Medal for rescuing the two-man crew of the Thames barge *Sepoy* off Cromer in 1933 after he drove the lifeboat onto the deck of the barge. (Painting by Charles Dixon, RA)

seamen in distress. Those who were chosen deserved every penny they received.

The earliest lifeboat crews had to put up with the most primitive of weatherproof clothing – canvas coated in linseed oil or tar – beneath which water would invariably find a way and soak any woollen undergarment. Occasionally crewmen would die of cold and exhaustion, but it is remarkable how much they were able to bear, hardened, as many of them were, to the fisherman's harsh life at sea.

One essential group, often overlooked, were those who helped to launch the lifeboats from their carriage off the beach. Even if horses were available, it was bound to involve a drenching in the surf, but when only human power was available it would necessitate launchers wading out with a rope up to their necks in water. And in

Launch of the Bridlington lifeboat George and Jane Walker: *a cold and wet experience for launchers and horses alike.*

Did you know?

Horses were usually volunteered by local farmers for launching the lifeboat. One horse at Hoylake, Cheshire, became so excited by the familiar sound of the maroon that it had a heart attack and died.

some of the remoter communities, it was the women who had to pull the lifeboat into and out of the water.

There was one famous launcher, Margaret Armstrong, who, by her 70th birthday in 1921, had not missed a launch of the lifeboat at Cresswell on the Northumberland coast for fifty years. In that time she had lost her father, three brothers and her son to fishing accidents at sea. In her early twenties, in

Launch of Padstow lifeboat in Harlyn Bay.

Did you know?
English oak, African mahogany, Burmese teak and Western red cedar were all used in the construction of a wooden lifeboat.

January 1876, she and other local women waded into the sea in an attempt to reach survivors aboard a Swedish ship aground, near Newbiggin. When this failed, Margaret set off on foot through a blizzard to alert the coastguard rescue team. She made it through, almost speechless with exhaustion and with her feet bleeding. The Swedish crew were ultimately saved.

The chances of survival for any man thrown overboard from a lifeboat were never good, especially as most could not swim. The use of cork, so prevalent in the build of early lifeboats, eventually came to the aid of a lifeboatman overboard when the first inspector of lifeboats to be appointed by the RNLI, Captain John Ross Ward, RN, designed a cork lifejacket in 1854 for all his crews.

Although they were not that comfortable to wear, especially for a man at an oar,

Henry Freeman of Whitby, sole survivor of the lifeboat capsize in 1861, thanks to his cork lifejacket. (The Sutcliffe Gallery, Whitby)

Did you know?
Between 1854 and 1886 RNLI lifeboats launched 5,000 times and saved 12,000 lives. Lifeboats had capsized on 41 occasions and 76 lifeboatmen had lost their lives.

Coxswain Robert Harland of Whitby in 1934 with a young admirer. (Photo Press)

➤➤

All the crew of Padstow's pulling lifeboat Arab *scrambled clear after she was washed ashore having lost most of her oars while on a mission to the ketch* Peace and Plenty, *seen wrecked in the background. The eleven-man crew of the station's steam lifeboat,* James Stevens No. 4, *were not so fortunate; eight men were lost when she overturned going to the fishing vessel's aid.*

'I got out again and found Richard Robinson fairly done. He leaned heavily on my arm and I think he must have been suffocated. Another sea came and when it receded, he had disappeared and I never saw him again. While underneath I called out to my brother, 'Clasper!' – that is a sort of nickname we gave him – but I could get no answer.'

John Jackson, one of only two survivors from the Southport lifeboat after she capsized attending the *Mexico*, December 1886

their value was proved during an incident at Whitby in 1861. The town ran its own lifeboat, independent of the RNLI, although they were supplied with a few of Captain Ward's lifejackets. On 9 February the lifeboat was called out six times in a gale to the aid of a number of vessels in trouble at the harbour mouth. On her last mission she capsized and every member of her crew was drowned except Henry Freeman, the only man to be wearing a lifejacket.

An early motor lifeboat,
Margaret Harker-Smith,
battling heavy seas at
Whitby harbour mouth.

After the tragedy, Whitby chose to put its two lifeboats under the jurisdiction of the RNLI and Henry Freeman later became coxswain and a celebrated Yorkshire figurehead. He was twice awarded the Silver Medal for gallantry, once for his services on the day of the disaster and once, nineteen years later, when he launched four times into a hurricane, each time saving the crew of a foundering ship.

Other men of the Victorian era, less widely remembered, but equally gallant, include William Taylor, a coastguard officer of Dunny Cove, near Cork who, in the 1860s and 1870s, three times earned the RNLI Silver Medal when launching local boats to stranded ships' crews. Daniel Shea, first the coxswain of Padstow lifeboat, then chief officer of the coastguard there and holder of three Silver Medals, eventually drowned on the Doombar with four other lifeboatmen on another rescue mission in February 1867. Coxswain Sydney Harris of Gorleston in Norfolk is still the only man to have received five Silver Medals, all between 1905 and

Margaret Armstrong, legendary launcher of Cresswell, Northumberland, still pulling her weight at the age of 70.

◀◀
Volunteers reconstruct a 1903 Cornish lifeboat rescue.

◀
The Dunmore East lifeboat crew help survivors ashore from the wrecked Fethard lifeboat and from the Norwegian schooner they had tried to save in February 1914. The schooner ran aground on the South Keeragh Island, off County Waterford and nine of the lifeboat crew were lost. The survivors remained on the barren island for three days before they could be rescued. (Poole, Waterford)

39

1916 and all aboard pulling and sailing lifeboats which, by then, were beginning to give way to the new age of motorised boats.

Probably the most famous lifeboatman ever to take the helm was Henry Blogg of Cromer, Norfolk. In an extraordinary career which spanned 51 years, 38 of which were as coxswain, he was responsible for saving 873 lives and was awarded an unequalled three Gold and four Silver Medals. He first joined the crew in 1894, still in the days of oars and sail. His first Gold Medal was earned aboard the town's pulling lifeboat during the First World War in 1917, rescuing survivors from a Swedish ship blown to pieces by a German mine. His third Gold came after he went to the aid of a Second World War convoy in 1941, aground in a gale on Haisborough Sands. By then he had proved himself the master of the motor lifeboat and demonstrated its capabilities time and again in the most extreme conditions.

For all the death and destruction wrought during the First World War, it proved a rugged testing ground for the internal combustion engine. Tanks, aeroplanes, motor vehicles, all won their spurs amid the mayhem. So, too, did motor lifeboats.

The hospital ship *Rohilla*, laden with medical staff on a mission to embark the

wounded from the Western Front at Dunkirk in October 1914, was driven onto rocks near Whitby in a gale. Sixty people aboard were drowned almost immediately when the stern section broke away. Thirty-five more were miraculously rescued by one of the Whitby pulling lifeboats before she was too badly damaged to continue. When, after three whole days, the town's second lifeboat and two others from neighbouring stations were also defeated by the storm, Tynemouth's petrol-driven lifeboat, *Henry Vernon,* was called.

Never before had a lifeboat been asked to travel 45 miles by sea to a rescue, but she made it to Whitby in pitch darkness, due to wartime blackout, and in gale force winds. There, in fearful conditions, she was able to get alongside the wreck and take off the remaining survivors. This epic rescue,

A 37ft Oakley class lifeboat undergoes a self-righting trial using the new technique of shifting water ballast.

41

A self-inflating airbag was fitted to Watson and Barnett class lifeboats in the 1970s. Here, the Barra Island lifeboat R.A. Colby Cubbin No. 3 *is towed to safety after a bag saved her crew by righting her after a capsize in heavy seas in November 1979.*

which earned Gold Medals for Tynemouth coxswain Robert 'Scraper' Smith and the station's honorary superintendent Captain H.E. Burton, who accompanied the crew, demonstrated beyond doubt the superior capabilities of a motorised lifeboat.

'The lifeboat came off the top of one sea and dropped into the trough of the next with such a terrible thud that everyone thought the engines had gone through the bottom of the boat, but the motor mechanic reported: "All's well. After that she will go through anything." The coxswain had the whole crew in the after cockpit. After each sea had filled it he counted his men.'

Robert Mahony, Honorary Secretary of Ballycotton lifeboat station, in his account of the lifeboat's rescue of the crew of the Daunt Rock lightship, near Cork, February 1936

Did you know?
A nurse, Mary Roberts, rescued by the Whitby lifeboat from the *Rohilla* in 1914, had survived the sinking of the *Titanic* three years earlier.

Although the RNLI founder, Sir William Hillary, had advocated the use of steam-driven lifeboats as early as 1824, the Institution had allowed the age of steam to pass it by until as late as 1890 when the 50ft *Duke of Northumberland* came into being. This first steam lifeboat, propelled by water sucked in and pushed out by a

> *Walmer lifeboat returns after a rescue, presenting the recovery party with urgent work as she is turned broadside on to the beach.*

Did you know?

Between them, the crews of Margate and Ramsgate lifeboats brought 3,400 troops to safety from the Dunkirk beaches in 1940.

pump, surprised many by its seaworthiness and saw thirty-three years of service, first at Harwich, then Holyhead and finally New Brighton on Merseyside, by which time she had saved 295 people. Two more of the hydraulically driven type were built and three others which used a propeller. The problem with steam lifeboats was their weight and size which prevented them from being launched from a beach, requiring instead a mooring in sheltered waters.

However, without the inspiration of George Lennox Watson, a naval architect appointed to advise the RNLI in 1887, lifeboats might have remained without mechanical power for much longer. Watson had already won the admiration of lifeboat crews by designing a very stable 36ft pulling and sailing boat fitted with water

Coxswain Robert Smith of Tynemouth, hero of the 1914 Rohilla *rescue.*

Did you know?
Lifeboats were first seen on television in 1947 when a new Liverpool class replaced the sailing lifeboat at New Quay, Cardiganshire, which had been on station for 40 years.

The steam- and hydraulic-driven lifeboat City of Glasgow, stationed at Harwich between 1901 and 1917.

The 48ft Solent class R. Hope Roberts, which served four stations between 1969 and 1993: Rosslare Harbour, Fraserburgh, Galway Bay and Courtmacsherry Harbour. (Rick Tomlinson)

A wooden 48ft Oakley class, The Earl and Countess Howe, *in high seas out from her station at Yarmouth, Isle of Wight.*

An early twentieth-century motor lifeboat under construction.

ballast tanks, although not self-righting. He quickly became the driving force behind the adoption of steam power and by the turn of the century began experiments fitting a petrol engine into a conventional pulling and sailing hull.

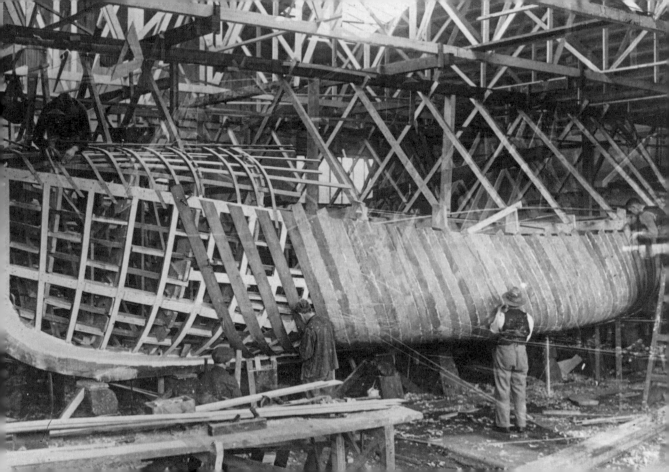

Watson died in 1904, but his successor and fellow pioneer James Rennie Barnett was ready to send a 38ft self-righter, equipped with a two-stroke Fay and Bowen engine, to Tynemouth for station trials in May 1905. At first, the Tynemouth crew refused to put to sea in a motor lifeboat, but through the enthusiasm of H.E. Burton, then a lieutenant with the Royal Engineers, who had to take the lifeboat to sea with a crew of his own sappers, the men of the station were eventually won round by the boat's capabilities. The trials proved that a lifeboat, still light enough to be launched from a slipway or carriage, could sustain a course directly into the wind and weather under mechanical power, something impossible under sail or with oars.

The early engines were not always reliable and the RNLI, while embarking on a programme of building petrol engine boats (thirteen had been built by the outbreak of the First World War), were at pains to point out that the motor was only an auxiliary to the sails. Nevertheless, steam power had had its short day and when, in 1923, the first twin-engined boat, the 60ft Barnett class, took up duty at New Brighton, trust in the internal combustion engine was absolute and the sail became no more than an occasional aid to stability or emergency means of propulsion.

Neither Watson's nor Barnett's motor lifeboat designs were self-righting, but their greater stability was considered more than ample compensation. The influence of these two men was such that by 1957, only six of the fleet of 178 lifeboats were self-righting. Capsizes still occurred, such as one at Fraserburgh in 1953 when six out of the lifeboat's seven-man crew drowned, trapped under the hull after she overturned in a heavy swell near the harbour mouth. In 1958 a new 37ft lifeboat, designed by Richard Oakley, was built. Not only was she able to right herself by transferring water ballast, if inverted, to a tank which pulled her back over, she also had greater stability than her non-self-righting predecessors.

The success of the Oakley system of self-righting and two more fatal capsizes to Watson class lifeboats (Longhope, Orkney, in 1969 and Fraserburgh, again, in 1970), convinced the RNLI to pursue a policy of ensuring new all-weather lifeboats should be built to right themselves.

Throughout the first half of the twentieth century the emphasis was on providing crews with lifeboats that could be launched at any state of the tide and in any weather, that had the reliability and seaworthiness to reach a casualty and the robustness to withstand the buffeting when going alongside. A ship aground would seldom break up immediately and her crew, however traumatised, could usually survive the wait for a 7, 8 or 9-knot lifeboat to make its steady way towards them.

But as the century progressed, new types of casualty presented themselves. In September 1930 the RNLI launched a lifeboat at Dover capable of 18 knots with twin 375hp engines. Although the design sacrificed some of the conventional lifeboat's all-weather capability, her speed was considered more important. This was in direct response to the growing number of passenger flights across the Channel. Only the year before, seven people had drowned off the Kent coast before rescuers could reach them, when an Imperial Airways plane bound for Paris crashed into the sea.

The US Coast Guard surf lifeboat upon which the RNLI's 15-knot Waveney class was based.

Did you know?

The first RNLI medal to be awarded for an inshore lifeboat rescue was the Bronze to the two-man crew of Amble's D class who saved two RAF men from the water after their motorboat had capsized in September 1969.

Although the *Sir William Hillary*, as this one-off was named, saw ten years' service at Dover, ironically, she was never called to a ditched aircraft. When the war arrived, the military took responsibility for air-sea rescue operations and the lifeboat

Peel's Atlantic 21 inshore lifeboat alongside a grounded fishing vessel in March 1980. Even though the bow section has been damaged and deflated, she is still able to operate in very difficult circumstances.

was sold to the Admiralty. The Second World War was an exceptionally busy time for RNLI crews who ran the added risk of encountering mines and enemy action on their missions to civilian and military casualties. Again reliability, not excessive speed, was what the crews were looking for and, in any case, the war stifled much new boat building, experimental designs in particular.

With the war over, the growing popularity of recreational sailing and water sports

maximum 9-knot speed, these lifeboats would risk arriving too late for a swimmer swept out to sea or the crew of a capsized sailing boat.

In 1963 the decision was taken to emulate a Brittany-based lifesaving society and place ten 16ft inflatable rescue boats close to a series of summertime resorts to provide a response to fast-developing incidents. The image of the RNLI was instantly transformed as these neoprene-covered nylon boats bounced across the waves at more than 20 knots with a two or three-man crew of young men, often with a water sports rather than the traditional fishing background.

While these small inflatable lifeboats quickly proved themselves an essential complement to the all-weather fleet, some of them remaining on station all year-

in post-war UK waters began to exercise the minds of those who ran the RNLI in the 1950s. They were beginning to find that their fleet of wooden lifeboats was not always appropriate for dealing with the dinghy sailor or holidaymaker in trouble. It could take half-an-hour to get the smallest lifeboat, the 35ft carriage-launched Liverpool class, to sea. With a

The Arun class not only gave speed but survivor capacity. Here, the Dover crew are able to land 183 passengers from the Hoverspeed ferry Princess Margaret *after she had hit the harbour entrance in March 1985. Four passengers lost their lives in the incident and the lifeboat hauled five people from the water. (C.P. Nelson)*

Did you know?
The French company Zodiac, the first commercial manufacturer of motorised inflatable boats, was originally a builder of airships.

round, further pioneering work was being done in the late 1960s and early 1970s by Rear Admiral Desmond Hoare, the headmaster of Atlantic College in South Wales. He developed a rigid hull version of an inflatable rescue boat which provided excellent seakeeping for a small, fast boat and the RNLI eagerly adopted the principle with its first 21ft, 29-knot inshore lifeboat, the Atlantic 21, entering service in 1972. Very soon the inflatable D class and the rigid inflatable Atlantic became the two

busiest types of lifeboat and their present-day successors, not greatly changed in appearance, are still the workhorses of the fleet.

The speed and versatility of the inshore boats was beginning to make some of the older, wooden lifeboats look cumbersome and only worth launching if the weather was really bad or the casualty far out to sea. At some stations, such as Aberystwyth in Wales where the first D class inflatable had been sent, the decision was taken to dispense with the big boat altogether as neighbouring stations could provide all-weather cover.

Again, the RNLI was to find inspiration from overseas in the quest to improve the response times of its offshore fleet. The US Coast Guard had developed a 44ft, steel 'surf' lifeboat which was self-righting and capable of 14 knots. The RNLI bought a new boat of this design from the Americans, subjected it to extensive tests around the shores of the UK and Ireland and, with the approval of many crews who tried it, started to build a version of the boat on the River Waveney at Lowestoft.

Twenty-two Waveney class boats were built in the next fifteen years, although they were only able to go to stations where they could be kept afloat at all times. Crews found her both robust and nimble and her revolutionary shape, a sharp 'V' at the bow and rounded at the stern, heralded the beginning of the end of the 150-year era of double-ended wooden-hull lifeboats.

By 1971 the RNLI had perfected its own design of fast lifeboat, the 52ft, 18-knot Arun class. Although the first two of her

The Arun class Charles Browne *served Buckie lifeboat station between 1984 and 2003. Here she comes in perilously close to the rocks to the aid of a fishing boat. (Alex Smith)*

Did you know?
When the last Arun lifeboat came out of RNLI service in February 2007, the class had launched 15,081 times and rescued 13,454 people.

Atlantic College in South Wales, where the rigid inflatable was first developed by Rear Admiral Desmond Hoare, later had its own Atlantic 21 lifeboat station manned by the students. Elisabeth Hostvedt, seen here at the bow, became the RNLI's first female crew member in 1969.

type had wooden hulls, she was designed to be built in glass-reinforced plastic (GRP). Not only could crews reach all compartments of the boat without receiving a soaking on deck for the first time, but the speed of the Arun gave them a far greater range of operation and usually less time away from work or home on a shout.

Hartlepool's 18-knot Arun class Keith Anderson. *(Peter Bentley)*

The RNLI's twenty-four-hour lifeboat service is only as good as its ability to get a lifeboat to sea at all states of the tide and in any weather. When the Waveney and Arun classes were introduced in the late 1960s and 1970s, with their extra speed and power, they could only be stationed where they could lie permanently afloat on a mooring. Their size and the shape of their hull and their exposed propellers were

A beach launch at Ilfracombe with the Mersey and the D class lifeboats.

An aluminium hull Mersey class under construction. Later models were built in fibre-reinforced composite. (Gilbert Hampton Photography)

Did you know?

It costs approximately £330,000 per day to run the RNLI. For every £1 spent, around 78p is spent on the rescue service, including the cost of the crew, the boats, the station properties and sea safety education; 19p is used for fundraising and 3p for support.

unsuitable at places where a slipway or a tractor and carriage were needed to get the lifeboat away.

The next challenge for the organisation was to design an all-weather lifeboat with the 18-knot speed of an Arun that could launch from a slipway or carriage, to replace the ageing and somewhat plodding Watson, Oakley and Rother-class lifeboats. It was no good being able to guarantee a

lifeboat would be on scene 30 miles out within two hours in some areas but not others – the standard of cover needed to be universal.

For slipway launches, the answer came with the development of the steel-built, 14.3m Tyne class which entered service in 1982. Designed to fit into existing boat-houses, she had a much squatter appearance than the Arun and her propellers were protected by substantial bilge keels. Her twin 425hp diesels gave her a top speed of 17 knots and an operating range of 240 nautical miles, allowing strategically placed stations such as the Lizard in Cornwall, Baltimore in County Cork, Longhope in Orkney and Bembridge on the Isle of Wight to offer a vastly improved service.

Six years after the Tyne class first appeared on the coast, the 12m Mersey class made

A Mersey-class on her carriage at Hastings. Note the shape of the hull which protects the propellers in shallow water.

Did you know?

In 2006, 51% of lifeboat launches were to leisure craft users, 29% to people not using any kind of craft, 12% to merchant or fishing vessels and 8% to other sea users.

its debut in 1988. She, too, was capable of 17 knots and had bilge keels to protect the propellers but, at 13 tonnes, was almost half the weight of the Tyne. This was necessary if she was to be towed successfully by tractor across the sand or shingle. Her light weight was achieved in the early boats by building the hull in aluminium and later, with the material tested for strength with brutal diligence, in fibre-reinforced composite (FRC). When the thirty-fourth Mersey took up duty at Aldeburgh in 1993, the Rother class she replaced was the last of the traditional double-ended lifeboats to be de-commissioned.

By this time work was well advanced in the quest to generate even greater power and speed in an all-weather lifeboat. There was always the danger of emergencies happening just out of the reach of the RNLI.

In September 1994, the car ferry *Estonia*'s bow doors were breached in violent seas in mid-Baltic and she sank claiming 852 lives. Her position, roughly 50 miles from any land, discouraged the authorities from calling on the Swedish or Finnish lifeboats. Had they been able to reach the scene to assist the rescue helicopters, it is likely many more lives would have been saved.

Although such emergencies are mercifully rare, the RNLI was determined to increase

'I didn't think the lifeboat was going to be able to get into the cave. I thought I was going to die because the cave was full up with water – I'm very thankful to the lifeboat crew.'

12-year-old surfer Chy Start-Walter after she had been rescued by the St Agnes inshore lifeboat from a cave on the Cornish coast

its radius of action and its capacity for survivors, should something similar occur in UK or Irish waters. With a 17m all-weather lifeboat, capable of 25 knots, it could do just that, promising to reach up to 50 miles from station – and within two hours in good weather. This was the Severn class which went on station first in 1996 and although she appeared to the unaccustomed eye to be just a slightly larger Arun, she actually represented a much greater advance in lifeboat technology. The power needed to increase maximum speed from 18 to 25 knots was three times that of the Arun. The FRC hull, while built for speed, needed to provide protection for the propellers against grounding and titanic strength to withstand the impact of a 41-tonne vessel hitting a wave at more than 20 knots. The design was a triumph of compromise, balancing

Thurso's Severn class lifeboat The Taylors negotiating storm force seas off Scotland's treacherous north coast. (Henrik Steffensen)

Did you know?
Lifeboats reach 95% of all casualties within 10 miles of the station in 30 minutes or less.

Self-righting trial of the first Tamar class lifeboat.

Bude's D class lifeboat tackling heavy Cornish surf. (Tim Martindale)

power with weight and seaworthiness with performance.

At the same time, the RNLI developed the Trent class, a 14m scaled-down version of the Severn with all the same attributes. By the time the build programme of these two classes was completed in 2004, sixty-eight lifeboat stations were equipped with them and the trusty Arun class had all but disappeared from the scene.

The latest design of an all-weather lifeboat is the Tamar class, the first of which went to Tenby in South Wales in April 2006. Just as with the step up from 9 to 18 knots came later with slipway launching boats, so it has with the Tyne replacement. This time,

with a 30-tonne weight and a wheelhouse designed to house the entire crew, slipways and boathouses have had to be rebuilt in preparation for the boat's arrival.

The crew of the 25-knot Tamar can control many of the lifeboat's functions remotely from the safety of their seats thanks to the computerised Systems and Information Management System (SIMS). Other features include advanced ergonomics and seating, which reduce the impact on the crew as the lifeboat crashes through waves, and a powered inflatable Y boat stored behind a hydraulic door at the stern to allow immediate deployment.

What of a successor to the carriage launched Mersey class? At the moment an experimental boat exists known simply as Fast Carriage Boat 2. If trials are successful, the RNLI could be operating sea-going water jet-propelled lifeboats echoing the early steam lifeboats of the late nineteenth century.

Meanwhile, the fleet of rigid inflatable B class Atlantics and 5m inflatable D class continue to perform miracles of manoeuvrability in the treacherous inshore waters they cover. The latest Atlantic is

The Tamar class, designed to launch from a slipway and to achieve a maximum 25 knots. (Derek King)

The prototype trials of a new carriage-launched lifeboat with water-jet propulsion.

8.5m, capable of 35 knots and is fitted with radar and VHF direction finding equipment and can be operated safely in daylight in a force 6/7 and at night in a force 5/6. Hundreds of people every year have an inshore lifeboat to thank for saving their lives and with increasingly sophisticated electronic paging systems for summoning crews, the RNLI's response to a call for help has never been more immediate.

>

Slipway launch of the Tamar at Padstow. (Nigel Millard)

The last time the RNLI's Gold Medal for bravery was awarded was for a rescue off the Shetland coast on 19 November 1997. Hewitt Clark, already the holder of one Silver and three Bronze Medals, drove the Lerwick Severn class lifeboat alongside the crippled cargo ship *Green Lily* within yards of the cliffs in a near hurricane to snatch five of her crew to safety. While assessing the situation, just before moving in for the rescue, he could not help remembering how, in very similar circumstances, the entire crew of the Penlee lifeboat had perished up against the Cornish cliffs sixteen years earlier.

Clark's major advantage was the power and agility of his lifeboat. The Penlee coxswain had only twin 60hp diesels aboard his 47ft Watson class with which to battle the elements. The Lerwick Severn's

Green Lily, moments after her crew had been taken off by helicopter and the Lerwick lifeboat. She very quickly began to break up.

twin diesels produced 2,400hp and, when expertly handled, could bring the lifeboat alongside, hold her in position and pull her away out of danger with split-second responsiveness.

His other great asset that day, although no less than was available aboard the Penlee boat, was the courage, strength and skill of his crew. Every man on board would have been able to take the helm if

required, operate the radio, the direction finder, the radar and the satellite navigation equipment, and be proficient in elementary first aid. At least two of them were qualified motor mechanics. As it happened, it was their dexterity and strength on deck, pulling survivors to safety, that was most valuable that day, but they were trained and ready for any eventuality. Tragically, the only man to lose his life on that fearsome day was the winchman of the HM Coast-

guard helicopter, Billy Deacon, with whom the lifeboat was working to save the *Green Lily*'s crew. He was swept off the deck of the wallowing ship seconds after he had seen the last of the survivors winched to safety aboard the helicopter.

Did you know?

When crew-member Robbie Maiden was washed off the deck of Hartlepool lifeboat at night in a Force 10 in February 1983, after 35 minutes in the sea, he was saved when a helicopter crew spotted the reflective strip on his lifejacket.

'One day you'll be battling with fog for twenty-two hours, looking for survivors and just as you're frozen stiff and giving up hope you spot them. Just the look on their faces when they realise they're not going to die.

That's enough.'

Joe Martin, former coxswain of Hastings lifeboat

It seems remarkable, with all the skills required to operate a modern lifeboat, that the RNLI can still rely primarily on volunteers to run and crew its 230 stations throughout the UK and Ireland. Nowadays there is no longer a pool of people to call on whose everyday job takes them to sea and much of the training, both basic and advanced, has to be supplied by the RNLI itself. Men and women of every occupation – teachers, builders, chefs, police officers, gardeners, solicitors – will be found on a modern lifeboat crew and although they might have had an affinity with the sea when they joined, many of the required skills would have been learned from scratch.

Every station with an all-weather lifeboat will have a full-time mechanic. At some of the more remote stations where employment is scarce, there will also be a full-time coxswain to ensure a twenty-four-hour response. Otherwise, crews on both the all-weather and inshore lifeboats give up their own time to the service. This does not just mean responding when the lifeboat is called out. Every week the lifeboat goes out on exercise to put the crew through its paces. In addition, volunteers must spend time in mobile training units, which tour the coast, learning electronic navigation, first aid and other skills. Most will also visit

Cleethorpes D class inshore lifeboat, another provided by Blue Peter *viewers. (Tom Collins)*

Trainees learn how to right a D-class inflatable in the Lifeboat College's sea survival centre. (Derek King)

the Lifeboat College at the RNLI's home in Poole, Dorset. Here they will benefit from specialist training facilities which include a wave pool (where you learn how to survive an inshore lifeboat capsize), a fire simulator, a full bridge simulator (for mission planning and execution in all weathers) and a live engine workshop.

An Atlantic 85 receives royal approval from the RNLI's patron, HM the Queen. Behind her, the RNLI president, HRH the Duke of Kent, speaks to crew members. (Derek King)

The dry suit does its job as New Brighton's Atlantic 75 takes a large wave. (New Brighton RNLI)

At many stations the crew still rely as much on their volunteer launching team as they do on their lifeboat for a successful mission, and tractor and carriage driving courses are run on the North Devon Coast for these vital links in the rescue chain. Other unsung volunteers at lifeboat stations such as the lifeboat operations manager (the person who decides to launch the lifeboat) will give up time to attend courses in Poole as well as ensuring a smooth-running station in an increasingly sophisticated world of search and rescue.

If the means of rescue are more sophisticated in the twenty-first century, the sea is still as ferocious an enemy to lifeboat crews as ever it was. When, in 2004, the Cleethorpes 16ft inflatable D class lifeboat *Blue Peter VI* (provided by the most recent BBC TV *Blue Peter* appeal) put out into a force 8 gale and heavy snow squalls, her four-man crew were doubtless grateful for their dry suits, lifejackets and pro-tective helmets. But the danger they faced, working with the Humber all-weather lifeboat, to rescue two men and their fishing boat before she was driven ashore, was as intense as any encountered by their oilskin-clad predecessors in a pulling boat.

When the four Cleethorpes men went to London to receive the medals awarded to them for their efforts (a Silver to Helmsman Gary Barlow and Bronze to the other three), one of them, Shaun Sonley, remarked to an interviewer: 'People ask why we do it, with the rough seas and everything. We get the best training and the best equipment, so you want to put it to good use.'

◄◄
Trained to perfection: Oban lifeboat crew present a reassuring sight. (Nigel Millard)

Did you know?

There are some 4,800 lifeboat crew members in the UK and Republic of Ireland. About 8% are women.

NEW AREAS FOR THE RNLI

With the annual running cost of the RNLI in excess of £100 million, it is remarkable that every penny required is still provided voluntarily by the public with no state funding whatsoever (apart from a small annual grant from the Irish Government). It is all the more impressive when you realise that in the past decade or so, the role of the lifeboat service has been expanding to do more than simply respond to emergencies around the coast.

In the past, when a member of the public or an under-prepared pleasure sailor found themselves in difficulties and in need of a lifeboat, the local newspaper or radio station would go to the coxswain after the rescue to try to draw some remark out of him about the foolhardiness of the person just returned to the shore. Although the press were seldom successful in eliciting criticism, some coxswains found it was an opportunity to put across some basic points about remaining safe at or by the sea.

The natural move for the RNLI was to launch its own sea safety initiative. It looked

at the most likely causes of mishaps, both to pleasure and to fishing and other small commercial craft and began to promulgate advice through pamphlets, boat show exhibitions and the media on how to prevent accidents at sea. Engine failure and ignorance of weather and tidal forecasts were major causes to be addressed. The internet has allowed many people to access the RNLI's safety advice in recent years and there is also a free service to pleasure-boat owners, known as 'Sea Check', whereby specially-trained volunteers will carry out an on-board safety consultation. Young people were also an important audience for the RNLI's safety messages, especially when it came to understanding the dangers of the seaside and the beach. This meant working closely with other beach safety organisations such as the

A jet-powered E class lifeboat for use on the Thames is put through its paces under Tower Bridge.

Did you know?
Nearly all of the 230 stations of the RNLI welcome visitors at certain times. Some are open all year and can accommodate pre-booked tours.

Did you know?

The RNLI operates 62 lifeguard units throughout the south-west of England. RNLI lifeguards saved 63 lives in 2006 and assisted 10,000 people altogether.

Maritime and Coastguard Agency, the Royal Life Saving Society and the Surf Life Saving Association of Great Britain (SLSA GB) to ensure a coordinated approach. This cooperation soon made it clear, particularly to the RNLI and SLSA GB, that it was not only in education and prevention of accidents that there was shared interest.

Both organisations were often called out to similar incidents off a beach in the summer and it made no difference to an exhausted swimmer or windsurfer whether they had been rescued by an RNLI inshore lifeboat or a lifeguard's inflatable rescue boat or jet-ski. It seemed illogical that they should not be fully coordinated. For that

'Mid-afternoon, we got a call to say that a fishing boat was suffering engine problems out at sea. It was a rough ride out, two and a half hours through strong winds and 5m waves. But one of the great things about the training is that the crew don't panic. They just get on with their jobs. After several attempts, we managed to secure a line to the fishing boat. The journey back was really intense – one lapse in concentration can lead to disaster.'

Coxswain David Steenvoorden of the Humber lifeboat

reason, and because the current lifeguard services were struggling for cash, the RNLI agreed in 2001 to take over responsibility for the lifeguards and their equipment on a number of the more popular West Country beaches, including all those on Cornwall's north coast. While the SLSA GB and its clubs still have the task of training surf lifesavers up to their Beach Lifeguard Award standard, the RNLI ensures that adequate practical lifesaving cover exists, ranging from clear safety information on the beach to lifeguard units fully equipped with all the paraphernalia required for surf rescue. Already, nearly 10,000 people receive some assistance every year, often in the face of considerable danger to rescuer and rescued alike.

Another question the RNLI began to ask itself in the late 1990s was where else to lend its lifesaving expertise and to provide cover. At several places on the coast the tide can recede for miles over shallow estuarial sand or mudflats. The 2004 tragedy at Morecambe in Lancashire when twenty cockle pickers lost their lives as the tide rose shows just how lethal these

areas can be. Even inshore lifeboats could often not get near to people stranded in such areas and so, in 2002, the first RNLI hovercraft went into action. There are four of these 8m craft in service at the moment at Southend in Essex, Hunstanton in Norfolk, New Brighton on Merseyside and at Morecambe. Their two to four-man

crews can cover shallow water, mudflats and sand at a maximum of 30 knots, making such tasks as shoreline searches particularly efficient.

Since 2002, the lifeboat service has also ventured inland for the first time. All the criteria for placing an inshore lifeboat on station on the coast – e.g. a busy

pleasure-boating area with high potential for accidents – existed at certain large inland areas of water. The RNLI now has a D class inflatable ready for boating mishaps on the Norfolk Broads and Atlantic 21s on Lough Erne in Northern Ireland and Lough Derg in the Republic of Ireland.

The River Thames in London is another new territory for the RNLI. There are

three stations – Gravesend, Tower Pier and Chiswick – which operate water jet-powered rigid inflatables, capable of 40 knots, making them the fastest lifeboats in the RNLI fleet. A fourth station up-river at Teddington operates two 5m D class lifeboats. The need for speed is essential on the Thames, where anyone in the water has little time to survive before being dragged under in the strong currents.

A surfer, rescued by Eastbourne inshore lifeboat crew, is placed in the care of the local mobile Coastguard unit. (Eddie Buckland)

The government-run coastguard service pre-dates the days of even the earliest lifeboats. It began in the late seventeenth century with mounted coastal patrols on the lookout for smugglers. It also had the responsibility for fending off looters and scavengers from the frequent shipwrecks. The service first became known as the Coast Guard in 1822 and, as the century progressed, took on the additional military role of providing a coastal blockade on behalf of the Admiralty.

All around the coast there were paid-off officers and men of the Royal Navy, working for the Coast Guard and often becoming involved in rescues. In 1854 the Coast Guard's role in lifesaving became more clearly differentiated from that of the RNLI when the Board of Trade issued every one of its outposts with rocket lines and ladders to bring shipwreck survivors ashore via breeches buoy. The RNLI would concentrate on rescue by means of lifeboat.

By the twentieth century the service, then known as HM Coastguard, had developed into the eyes and ears for all search-and-rescue missions around the coast of the United Kingdom. With the advent of radar, ship-to-shore radio and direction finding, the Coastguard stations and lookouts became an essential link between a casualty out to sea and those called to their assistance, especially RNLI lifeboats.

Nowadays, every rescue is coordinated by one of the nineteen Maritime Rescue Co-ordination Centres and in nearly all instances it will be the Coastguard which receives the initial distress call and activates the lifeboat station pagers and requests a launch. (An equivalent relationship exists between the Irish Coast Guard and RNLI stations in the Republic of Ireland.) The crews' pagers will tell them simultaneously that a request has been made and which

boat is required, ensuring that they can reach the boathouse, get kitted up and launch the lifeboat with minimum delay, frequently in less than ten minutes.

Joint exercise between Sunderland's Mersey class lifeboat and an RAF Sea King helicopter. (Sgt Rick Brewell ABIPP)

> *HM Coastguard, the eyes and ears for maritime rescue.*

Did you know?

When the Republic of Ireland became independent in 1921, its lifeboat stations remained in the care of the RNLI, which they still are to this day.

Often, these days, a lifeboat will be working in conjunction with a search-and-rescue helicopter. The Maritime and Coastguard Agency itself operates four Sikorsky S61N which are standing by and, in daytime, able to get airborne within fifteen minutes

◄
A Royal Navy Sea King from RNAS Culdrose exercises with the Port Isaac D class off the Cornish coast.

▲
The RAF and Bangor Atlantic 21 train together off the Northern Ireland coast. (Tracey Mitchell)

of being scrambled. The RAF and the Royal Navy both have search-and-rescue (SAR) Sea King helicopters available to cover the rest of the UK coast with a similar response time. Lifeboat crews exercise regularly with their local SAR helicopters, practising coordinated searches and techniques for winching survivors from the deck.

Did you know?
The Sikorsky S61N
search-and-rescue
helicopter operated
by the Maritime and
Coastguard Agency
can carry up to 20
survivors.

If this story has demonstrated the RNLI's need always to work closely with other agencies concerned with the welfare of seafarers around these shores, it has also shown how other countries' lifeboat services have played an important part in the Institution's success. The French inspired the adoption of the inflatable as a rescue boat and the

Americans the first fast all-weather lifeboat. An International Maritime Rescue Federation exists to help countries exchange lifesaving technology and ideas and further the cause in less well-developed countries. The RNLI may be marginally the oldest member of this federation, but it is not the only one relying entirely on voluntary contributions. The Dutch lifeboat service was founded a few months later than the RNLI in 1824 and, along with the Germans and the Swedes is run as a charity, independent of the state. Others, such as the French sea rescue society, receive some government money but raise voluntary funds as well. In America, the US Coast Guard, with its military as well as its life-saving role, is a state-run concern.

Some countries from other continents have modelled their own, more recently formed sea-rescue services on the volunteer

Did you know?
The RNLI operates a rapid response unit which sends inflatables and crews to flood disasters worldwide. It was last used abroad in February 2005 in Guyana, South America.

systems of European countries. In South Africa, Uruguay and Chile lifeboat services are dependent on volunteer crews and fundraising techniques reminiscent of the RNLI. Each of these countries operates lifeboats that first saw service with the RNLI and many others around the world including Australia, New Zealand and China – which recently took delivery of seven ex-RNLI Aruns – are also giving extended useful service to boats no longer required in UK waters.

Here is a typical incident involving a modern lifeboat recounted from both the coxswain's and survivor's point of view:

Location: The Argyll coast, off Oban
Date: 17 December 2005

The engine of the yacht *Classic Wave* cuts out just as she is passing between the isles of Kerrera and Bach off Oban. Her skipper, Bob Hartley recalls: 'We got the foresail up but it wasn't enough to keep us clear and we went aground.'

He makes a precautionary call to the coastguard believing she will refloat on the turning tide, but the Oban Trent class lifeboat is called out just in case. She arrives on scene within a few minutes under the command of Coxswain Ronnie MacKillop.

By now the yacht is taking on water in a 3m swell and the lifeboat edges into the shallows close enough for crew-member Peter MacKinnon to climb aboard with a salvage pump. But the pump can't cope with the amount of water flooding through the damaged hull; it is time for him and the three yachtsmen to abandon ship.

Now in driving rain and strong wind, with waves giving a rise and fall of 3m between the two decks, the coxswain manoeuvres back alongside the yacht and one of her crew leaps aboard. Such a leap is beyond the two older remaining yachtsmen so the lifeboat crew prepare their liferaft to use as a ferry between the two vessels.

Suddenly the yacht comes free from the rocks and immediately her hull disappears beneath the water. The two

Baltimore lifeboat prepares to pick up crew who have leapt overboard from a sinking freighter off the southern Irish coast.

The yacht Bacarole *about to sink in a Force 9 in Porth Cressa Bay, Isles of Scilly, on 12 September 1993. Coxswain Barry Bennett of St Mary's lifeboat earned the RNLI Bronze Medal after he steered the lifeboat into very shallow water so that his crew could haul the lone yachtsman to safety just before the yacht went down.*

Survivors safe aboard Courtmacsherry Harbour lifeboat after they had been rescued from their yacht, Supertaff, *in storm force winds off Ireland's southern coast in October 1998. Second Coxswain Daniel O'Dwyer was awarded the RNLI Bronze Medal for this rescue.*

Fifty-one passengers were winched to safety from the Dutch sail training schooner, *Eendracht, after she was swept on to a sandbank in a gale after leaving Newhaven harbour in October 1998. Newhaven's Arun class lifeboat was in attendance throughout the operation.*

RN helicopter and Port Isaac D class to the rescue of two canoeists in trouble on Cornwall's north coast. (Colin Shephard, The Mirror)

When the fishing vessel Zuider Zee fouled her propellers with her nets, Skegness Mersey class was called urgently to take her in tow to safety. (Hunstanton RNLI)

Rescued in the nick of time: St Mary's lifeboat from the Isles of Scilly get alongside the stricken French trawler Sauveterre and takes off her crew before she sinks. (Steve Farrall)

yachtsmen are able to grab the liferaft and are swept clear, but lifeboatman Peter MacKinnon is being pulled down with the sinking yacht. He fights desperately to regain the surface. His coxswain recalls: 'I was absolutely terrified for his safety but you just have to steel yourself and get on with it.'

To his utter relief he sees the yacht's own liferaft inflate automatically and his crewman clutches hold of it. Soon all three men are safely aboard the lifeboat.

Bob Hartley reflected afterwards: 'I always believed in the RNLI but I never thought I would have to use them. They saved our lives. At no time did we feel desperate – we felt the lifeboat was in control. It was all so quick. We went aground at 12.15 p.m. and were back in Oban two hours later.' Coxswain Ronnie

MacKillop said afterwards: 'At the end of the day we lost a salvage pump [replaced later by the yacht's insurers], but that's a small price to pay. You have to trust your training and your instincts and the boys who are with you.'

A teenage holidaymaker caught by the tide on rocks at Newquay, Cornwall, in July 2005, is helped aboard the town's D class lifeboat. (Chrissie Laming, Newquay Voice Newspaper)

TAMAR

The Tamar class lifeboat is the RNLI's latest design and will gradually replace the Tyne class. She is bigger and faster than the Tyne and can be launched from a slipway or lie afloat. The Tamar includes the computerised Systems and Information Management System (SIMS) that enables crew to control many of the lifeboat's functions remotely from the safety of their seats. Other features include advanced ergonomics that reduce the impact on the crew as the lifeboat crashes through waves, and a powered Y boat stored behind a transom door to allow immediate deployment. The first Tamar went on station at Tenby in Wales in 2006.

Category:	All weather
Introduced:	2006
Length:	16m
Range:	250 nautical miles
Speed:	25 knots
Weight:	31.5 tonnes
Crew:	6
Construction:	Fibre-reinforced plastic (FRP)
Launch type:	Slipway or afloat

SEVERN

The Severn class lifeboat was introduced in 1995 and shares the same hull shape as the Trent class. She carries a powered Y boat that can be launched and recovered by a lightweight crane to enable rescues close to shore. Her propellers are protected so she can take ground without damage.

Category:	All-weather
Introduced:	1995
Length:	17m
Range:	250 nautical miles
Speed:	25 knots
Weight:	41 tonnes
Crew:	6
Construction:	Fibre-reinforced composite (FRC)
Launch type:	Moored afloat

TRENT

The Trent class lifeboat is designed to lie afloat, either at deep-water moorings or at a berth. Introduced in 1994, she shares the same hull shape as the Severn class but is a smaller version. The sheerline sweeps down for ease of survivor recovery. As with the Severn, her propellers are protected so she can take ground without damage.

Category:	All-weather
Introduced:	1994
Length:	14m
Range:	250 nautical miles
Speed:	25 knots
Weight:	27.5 tonnes
Crew:	6
Construction:	FRC
Launch type:	Moored afloat

TYNE

The Tyne class lifeboat was the first 'fast' slipway lifeboat. She is the RNLI's main slipway-launched lifeboat, but can also lie afloat. Features include a low-profile wheelhouse and a separate cabin behind the upper steering position. The propellers are protected by substantial bilge keels. The last Tyne was built in 1990 and the class will be gradually replaced by the Tamar class.

Category:	All-weather
Introduced:	1982
Length:	14m
Range:	240 nautical miles
Speed:	17 knots
Weight:	25 tonnes
Crew:	6
Construction:	Steel hull, aluminium wheelhouse
Launch type:	Slipway or afloat

MERSEY

The Mersey class lifeboat was introduced in 1988 and was the RNLI's first 'fast' carriage lifeboat. She was designed to be launched from a carriage, but can also lie afloat or be launched from a slipway. Propellers are protected by partial tunnels and substantial bilge keels. The last Mersey was built in 1993.

Category:	All-weather
Introduced:	1988
Length:	12m
Range:	145 nautical miles
Speed:	17 knots
Weight:	13 tonnes
Crew:	6
Construction:	Aluminium or FRC
Launch type:	Carriage, afloat or slipway

ATLANTIC 75 AND 85

B Class

The Atlantic 85 is a rigid inflatable life-boat, introduced in 2006 as the latest development of the B class. She has a manually operated self-righting mechanism and is capable of being beached in an emergency without sustaining damage to engines or steering gear. The Atlantic 85 is fitted with radar and VHF direction finding equipment and can be operated safely in daylight in a force 6/7 and at night in a force 5/6. The details given are for the Atlantic 85 introduced in 2006.

Category:	Inshore
Introduced:	1972 (latest version 2006)
Length:	8.3m
Range:	2½ hours at maximum speed
Speed:	35 knots
Weight:	1.9 tonnes
Crew:	3/4
Construction:	FRC hull with inflatable sponsons
Launch type:	Trolley, floating boathouse or davit

D class

The D class has been the workhorse of the service for more than forty years. She is small and highly manoeuvrable, making her ideal for rescues close to shore in fair to moderate conditions. She has a single outboard engine and can be righted manually by the crew following a capsize. The design of the D class has continued to evolve since her introduction. The details given are for the latest version that was introduced in 2003.

Category:	Inshore
Introduced:	1963 (latest version in 2003)
Length:	5m
Range:	3 hours at maximum speed
Speed:	25 knots
Weight:	338kg
Crew:	2/3
Construction:	Hypalon coated polyester
Launch type:	Trolley or davit

➤

The crew of the St Agnes D class inflatable tackle the north Cornish surf. (Kirsten Prisk)

The RNLI Heritage Trust has been set up to preserve the history of the RNLI by caring for objects and the archives that tell the story of the service since 1824. In addition to its collections and archives at RNLI headquarters in Poole, Dorset, it runs a number of museums round the coast. For details, see below:

GRACE DARLING MUSEUM

Radcliffe Road, Bamburgh,
Northumberland
NE69 7AE
Tel: 0845 122 6999

Nearest RNLI station: Seahouses
Commemorates the life of Victorian Britain's greatest heroine and the story of the wreck of the SS *Forfarshire* in 1838. North Region/Northumberland

Nearest major town: Alnwick/Berwick-upon-Tweed
Nearest train station: Berwick-upon-Tweed

RNLI HENRY BLOGG MUSEUM

The Rocket House, The Gangway, Cromer, Norfolk NR27 9ET
Tel: 01263 511294

Henry Blogg's famous lifeboat H.F. Bailey on display at the museum in Cromer. (Charter Consultant Architects)

Nearest RNLI station: Cromer
Celebrates one of the bravest men who ever lived; the most highly-awarded lifeboatman who helped to save 873 lives. East Region/Norfolk
Nearest major town: Norwich
Nearest train station: Cromer

RNLI WHITBY MUSEUM
Pier Road, Whitby YO21 3PU
Tel: 01947 602001

Nearest RNLI station: Whitby
A classic Victorian double-boathouse home of the 1919 lifeboat *Robert and Ellen Robson* and the dramatic story of lifesaving in Whitby.
North Region/Yorkshire
Nearest major town: Whitby
Nearest train station: Whitby

➤
A rocket and line rescue team uses a breeches buoy to bring off the crew of the German sailing ship, Adolf Vinnen, *wrecked at The Lizard in February 1923.*

RNLI HISTORIC LIFEBOAT COLLECTION, CHATHAM HISTORIC DOCKYARD

Lifeboat!,The Historic Dockyard, Chatham, Kent ME4 4TZ
Tel: 01634 823800

Nearest RNLI station: Sheerness
The RNLI's national collection of seventeen history-making lifeboats from pulling-sailing days to the Arun class.
SE Region/Kent
Nearest town: Chatham
Nearest train station: Chatham

RNLI ZETLAND MUSEUM

The Esplanade, Redcar, Cleveland
TS10 3AH
Tel: 01642 494311

Nearest RNLI station: Redcar
Home of the Zetland, the world's oldest
surviving lifeboat, built in 1802.
North Region/Redcar and Cleveland
Nearest town: Redcar
Nearest train station: Redcar

RNLI HEADQUARTERS: COLLECTIONS AND ARCHIVES

West Quay Road, Poole, Dorset BH15
1HZ
Tel: 01202 662228

Nearest RNLI station: Poole
Houses RNLI object collections in store,
the library and archive.Visits by researchers
welcome by appointment.
SW Region/Dorset
Nearest town: Poole
Nearest train station: Poole

1772 Crewe Trust established for the benefit of those shipwrecked on the Northumberland coast.

1777 Earliest record of a boat kept specifically for rescuing the shipwrecked at Formby, Lancashire.

1786 Lionel Lukin builds the first unsinkable, purpose-designed rescue boat for the Crewe Trust.

1789 Launch of Greathead's 'Original' lifeboat, based partially on William Wouldhave's model.

1824 Sir William Hillary's National Institution for the Preservation of Life from Shipwreck is founded.

1838 Grace Darling and her father carry out their famous rescue of survivors of the *Forfarshire*, wrecked on the Farne Islands.

1851 Duke of Northumberland becomes President of RNLI and launches competition for best new model of a lifeboat.

1854 RNLI accepts annual grant from government.

1854 Cork lifejackets first issued to lifeboat crews.

1869 RNLI regains independence from state.

1886 Twenty-seven lifeboatmen lost from the Southport and St Anne's lifeboats.

1890 Launch of first steam-driven lifeboat.

1891 First Lifeboat Saturday fundraising event held in Manchester.

1905 First station trials of a petrol engine in a lifeboat at Tynemouth.

1914 Capabilities of motor lifeboats proven during *Rohilla* rescue at Whitby.

1924 First international lifeboat conference held in London.

1941 Coxswain Henry Blogg of Cromer wins his third Gold Medal going to the aid of a stranded wartime convoy.

1948 The first joint mission of a lifeboat and helicopter to deliver emergency rations to stranded keepers of the Wolf Rock lighthouse.

1956 VHF radio introduced aboard lifeboats.

1958 Self-righting lifeboats reintroduced into RNLI fleet with the 37ft Oakley class.

1963 Inflatable inshore lifeboats introduced into RNLI fleet.

1967 The first 'fast' all-weather lifeboat, the 15-knot Waveney class, enters service.

1971 The first 18-knot Arun class built.

1972 First rigid inflatable Atlantic class lifeboat enters service.

1996 RNLI launches its sea safety campaign.

1996 25-knot all-weather Severn and Trent class lifeboats introduced.

1997 The most recent Gold Medal (and the first since the Penlee disaster in 1981) awarded to Coxswain Hewitt Clark of Lerwick.

2001 RNLI takes responsibility for beach lifeguards in south-west England.

2002 First RNLI rescue hovercraft enters service.

2004 HM The Queen officially opens the Lifeboat College at Poole, Dorset.

2007 RNLI announces its busiest year ever in 2006, with lifeboats launching on average 23 times a day with 8,015 people rescued in total. The year also sees a record income of £126.8 million.